DATE DUE

FEB 06 2006		
FEB 3 1997		NOV 25 2012
FEB 01 1999		
12/19		
FEB 05 2003		
JAN 27 2004		
JAN 09 2006		
MAR 17 2009		

Demco, Inc. 38-293

About the Book

What is a star? Why do stars twinkle? Why do we see stars only at night? What are they made of? What is the difference between a star and a planet?

The fascination of the sky at night — its vastness and its mysterious quality of the unknown — makes stars a perfect subject for young boys and girls. Everyone, no matter where he or she lives, has experienced the wonder of a nighttime sky and asked questions. Melvin Berger attempts to answer the questions most asked by young children and to stimulate other ideas and discussions.

Dramatic, vivid illustrations by Marilyn Miller convey the vastness and the beauty of our universe.

Every *Science Is What and Why* book is checked for scientific accuracy by an expert.

STARS

BY MELVIN BERGER
ILLUSTRATED BY MARILYN MILLER

COWARD McCANN & GEOGHEGAN, INC.   NEW YORK

General Editor: Margaret Farrington Bartlett
Consultant: Theodore D. Johnson
Montclair Public Schools

Text copyright © 1971 by Melvin Berger
Illustrations copyright © 1971 by Marilyn Miller

Library of Congress Catalog Card Number: 78-132593
PRINTED IN THE UNITED STATES OF AMERICA
06209
Second Impression

"Twinkle, twinkle, little star,
How I wonder what you are."

Have you ever heard these words?
They are from an old, old song.
People have always wondered about stars.
Have you ever wondered —
— how big are the stars?
— what are they made of?
— how far away are they?
— why do they shine?
— what makes them twinkle?

The stars that you see on a clear, dark night
are not little at all.
Each star is much bigger than our earth.
Stars are so big that one million earths —
or even more —
could easily fit inside most stars.

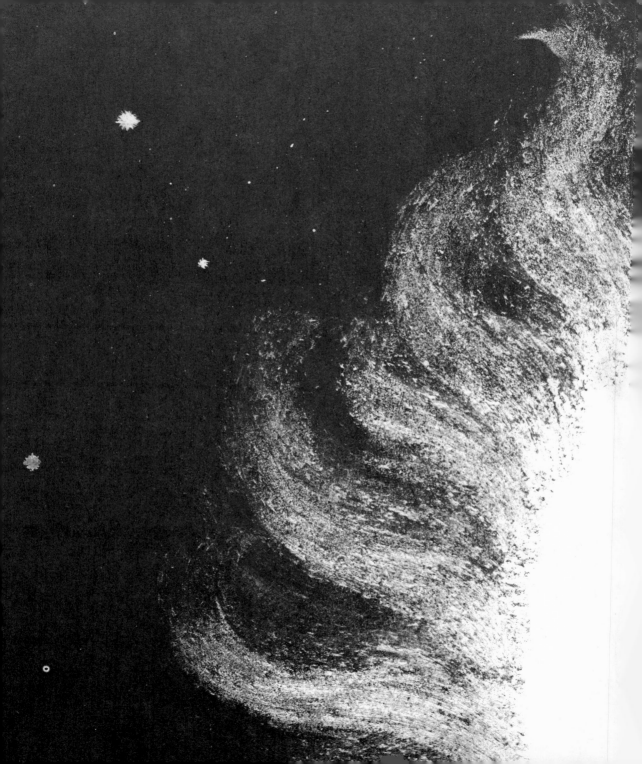

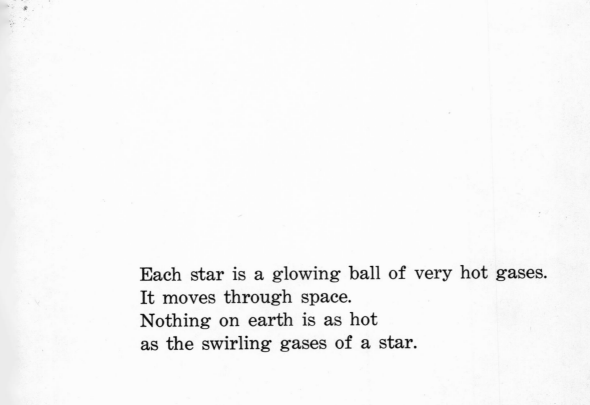

Each star is a glowing ball of very hot gases.
It moves through space.
Nothing on earth is as hot
as the swirling gases of a star.

Both the earth and the stars move in space.
But they are not the same.
Stars are much bigger than the earth.
Stars shine and give off light.
The earth does not make any light of its own.
The stars make heat.
They are much hotter than the earth.

The earth is a planet.
Planets orbit, or travel, around a star.
Our planet earth
orbits around a star.
This star is the sun.

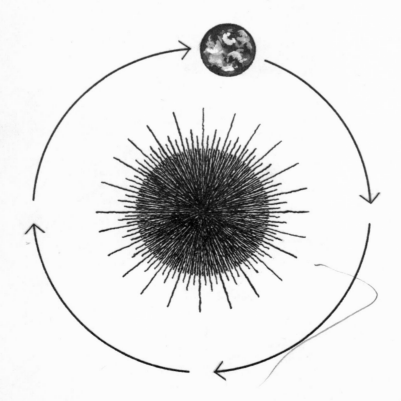

The other stars are similar to the sun.
But our sun is much, much, **much** closer to the earth
than any other star.

Imagine that you could take a walk in space.
Each step would carry you 93,000,000 miles.
With one giant step you would reach the sun,
which is 93,000,000 miles away.

After a whole day of "walking"
you would reach some of the other stars —
billions and trillions of miles out in space.

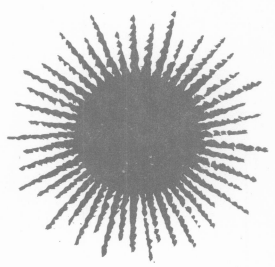

Because the sun is so close
you can feel its heat.
You can be blinded by its light.

Other stars are also hot and bright,
but they are so far away from the earth
that you cannot feel their heat.
You only see their light
as little points that twinkle in the night.

The gases which make up the star
make the heat and light.
Most of the gas is hydrogen.
The heat of the stars
makes the atoms of hydrogen
move and jump about with great energy.
They keep bumping into one another.
Sometimes they bump very hard
and they stick together.
Each time this happens
they change some of their energy into heat and light.
A burst of heat and a flash of light
are sent out in all directions.

This is happening
to so many hydrogen atoms all the time
that the stars give off
a steady stream of heat and light.

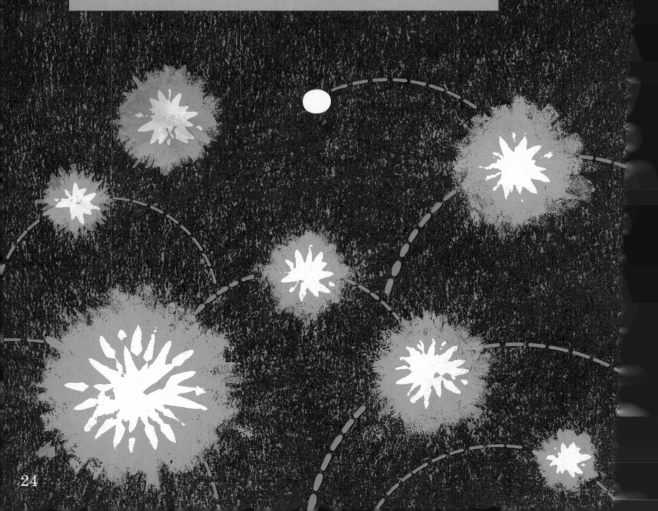

Why does the steady light from the stars
seem to twinkle?

Light from the stars
passes through the layers of air around the earth
before you see it.
The moving layers of air
bend and break the light.

It is similar to looking at your big toe
while you are swimming or taking a bath.
The moving water
keeps changing the appearance of your toe,
even though your toe does not change.
In the same way
the moving air
makes the stars seem to be twinkling,
even though their light is steady.

As you look at your toe in the water,
it also seems to be changing its shape.
It gets long and short,
skinny and fat,
as the water moves.

The same thing happens with the stars.
The moving layers of air make stars look pointed.

All the stars send out light all the time,
but we cannot always see their light.
During the day
the light from the nearby sun makes the sky so bright
that it hides the light from the faraway stars.

Sometimes clouds also hide
the light from the stars.

But on a clear night
the wonder of the stars is there for all to see.

On clear, dark nights during the summer or fall
you can see a large group of stars
over one part of the sky.
The stars seem so close together
that they form a white band across the sky.
Someone once thought
that it looked like a milk-white road.
Since then this group of stars
has been called the Milky Way.

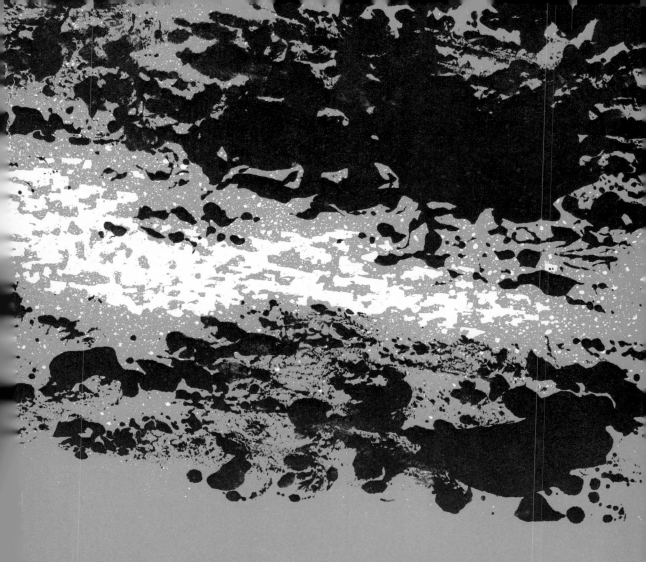

The Milky Way is a group of about 100 billion stars.
Such a group or family of stars
is called a galaxy.
The sun is one of the stars
in the Milky Way galaxy.

Our Milky Way galaxy is shaped like a gigantic pinwheel.
Most of the stars are clustered in the center part.
The rest are scattered in the arms
that come out from the center.

Just as a pinwheel spins in the wind,
so our galaxy,
with all its stars,
spins in space.

Since the earth is a planet of the sun,
it travels through space with the sun.
At the same time
the earth turns around itself once a day.
It also moves in an orbit around the sun once a year.

Because the earth is turning and orbiting,
the stars seem to be moving across the sky.
You see the sun rise in the morning
and set at night.
You see the other stars rise in the evening
and set at dawn.
And all of them rise and set
at different places in the sky
during the different seasons of the year.

Man has put the movement
of the sun and stars to good use.
He uses the movement of the sun
across the sky
to mark the hours and days.

He uses the different positions
of the stars in the sky
to mark the seasons and the years.

And he uses some stars,
such as the North Star,
to guide ships and planes on long trips.

Our eyes can see about 2,000 stars
on a dark, clear night.
Most are stars in our galaxy.
With a telescope we can see many more stars.
We can also see many other galaxies.
Each of these galaxies
has billions and billions of stars.

The next time that you sing "Twinkle, twinkle,"
think of the wonders of the stars.
Each star is like the sun,
an immense ball of hot, glowing gas.
It is billions and trillions of miles to the stars.

The hydrogen atoms
that make up the stars come together,
sending out streams of heat and light.
There are billions of stars in our galaxy
and billions of galaxies in space.
The stars and planets move through space
at hundreds of miles a second.

Look at the sky on a clear night
and watch the billions of stars
out in space.

About the Author

Melvin Berger presently lives in Great Neck, New York, with his family. He teaches science in the Plainview public schools.

A graduate of the University of Rochester, he did graduate work at Teacher's College, Columbia University, and at the University of London in England.

Mr. Berger is the author of ATOMS in the *Science Is What and Why* series plus three science books for boys and girls and a number of scientific articles for magazine publication.

The Artist

Though Marilyn Miller is an old hand at practically all phases of art (lettering, oils, etching, slide films, fashion art, poster, etc.) her illustrations for THE TIDE have all the freshness and enthusiasm of a brand-new talent.

Miss Miller has illustrated many books for children, in addition to her free-lance work for the United Nations, Ford, *Harper's*, the New York *Times*, and many other sources. She received her training at the California School of Fine Arts and the Art Students League of New York.

She and her husband, with their three children, live and work in a glass and redwood house deep in the woods of Connecticut.